Uplifting words

Popular Quotes & Biblical-Inspired words of wisdom

R. D. Garland

Table of Contents

Chapter 1: The Value of Happiness……………..4

Chapter 2: Perseverance & Togetherness………17

Chapter 3: Overcoming Fear……………….......35

Chapter 4: Strength…………………………….51

Chapter 5: What Does Love Look Like? 63

Chapter 6: Dealing With Pain…………………...76

Chapter 7: Having Faith………………………87

Acknowledgements………………………….103

Citations……………………………………...104

Foreword: There is nothing more empowering than a good quote to liven your spirits for the day. Whether you're a male or a female, young or old, I believe that these quotes can be helpful for you or perhaps someone you know that is going through tough times. An encouraging word, coupled with an inspirational picture can help someone you love more than you know.

Chapter 1
The Value of Happiness

"Success is not valued by how much money you make or what kind of cars you drive; it is valued by your happiness. Once we get back to the faith we'll be a lot happier, because we're renting all the things we have in this life while we're here anyway."[i]

-Martin Lawrence

"Love is that condition in which the happiness of another person is essential to your own."

-Robert A. Henlein

"Delight yourself in the LORD and He will give you the desires of your heart."
-Psalm 37:4

My two cents: We seem to mistakenly substitute Gods' presence in our lives with obtaining material things. Those items will not last forever. Even a beautiful ring will eventually tarnish, but Gods' love is eternal.

Notes:
_____
_____
_____

"Life is not always about fulfilling our own selfish desires; it is about pleasing God and allowing Him to see that we love Him more than we love ourselves. Take care of your fellow neighbors. That's a good way to start."

"It is impossible to constantly strive to be like them and still be you in the end."

"And above all these put on love, which binds everything together in perfect harmony."
-Colossians 3:14

"Our prime purpose in this life is to help others, and if you can't help them, at least don't hurt them."[ii]
-Mohandas Gandhi

"This is my commandment, that you love one another as I have loved you."
-John 15:12

My two cents: We have to put away our petty differences and start to redefine how we think about what happiness is. It is amazing how much happiness comes from helping others.

Notes:

_____
_____
_____

"Whatever you believe is what you will receive. To achieve greatness, you must believe that you are great and that you deserve to be great. There's absolutely nothing you cannot achieve if only you believe."
-Sherona Nandram

"Don't cry because it's over. Smile because it happened."[iii]
-Dr. Seuss

"But even if you should suffer for righteousness' sake, you will be blessed. Have no fear of them, nor be troubled…"
-1 Peter 3:14

"We are what we repeatedly do. Excellence then, is not an act, but a habit."
-Aristotle

"If you want an empty life, fill it with yourself. If you want a full life, empty yourself and fill your heart and your life with elements that will benefit others.

"A glad heart makes a cheerful face, but by sorrow of heart the spirit is crushed."
-Proverbs 15:13

<u>*My two cents*</u>: So many people base their happiness on the way other people feel, but that type of thinking is what keeps us from being happy. When it comes to *your* happiness, it all starts with 'you,' literally. So, stop letting your happiness lie in the hands of others. Own your happiness.

Notes:
___
___
___

"Giving 100% effort in a relationship means loving each other when you may not particularly like each other at the moment."

"Happiness is not something you postpone for the future; it is something you design for the present."[iv]
                                             -Jim Rohn

"Positivity has a lot to do with your overall success in life. Think about a job interview! It's not about proving that you already know what YOU can do, but what you are capable of with God!"

"Happiness is a journey, not a destination."[v]
                                             -Ben Sweetland

"There is more happiness in giving than there is in receiving."
-Acts 20:35

My two cents: So many of us look for our happiness in the things we possess. However, as you get older and the things you once revered more than God start to become more meaningless, money is no longer your God, and your family is like gold. Cherish the small things now, because in the end they will be the only things that matter.

Notes:
_____
_____
_____

"When it comes to positivity, sometimes the only positive things you will hear about you comes from yourself[vi]."

"When a person has an abundance, his life does not result from the things he possesses."

"The happiest people don't necessarily have the best of everything they just make the best of everything they have."[vii]

-Unknown

"A joyful heart is good medicine, but a crushed spirit dries up the bones."
-Proverbs 17:22

<u>***My two cents***</u>: It doesn't cost anything to be happy. True happiness starts with your attitude. So, try to not take everything so seriously. Live life as if tomorrow was not promised, because it's not. Have fun and enjoy each moment for it is a gift from God.

Notes:
_____
_____
_____

"Happy wife, happy life."

-Any smart man

"Don't just let happiness happen on accident. Do it purposefully."

"He who finds a wife finds a good thing and obtains favor from the Lord."

-Proverbs 18:22

"Steadfast love and faithfulness meet; righteousness and peace kiss each other."
-Psalm 85:10

My two cents: There is no greater happiness than that found in being married. It is challenging no doubt, but the rewards are far greater than the struggles. It is a journey that is unlike any other and the lessons learned help you develop into a stronger person. The happiness you feel after being with someone for an extended period of time is unmatched.

Notes:

_____
_____
_____

"Happy are those hearing the word of God and keeping it!"
-Luke 11:28

"If you look for happiness in the opinions of others, the reflection you see will never be correct. Until you focus on your own happiness, you will never be satisfied."

"Make the rest of your life the best of your life."
-Eric Thomas

"Therefore my heart is glad, and my whole being rejoices; my flesh also dwells secure."
-Psalm 16:9

<u>*My two new cents*</u>: Life is not always about focusing on what other people think about you. Once you realize that your happiness is solely dependent upon what gives you enjoyment, you will realize more people see you being happy, compared to when their opinions made you feel that way.

Notes:
_____
_____
_____

"In order to carry a positive action we must develop here a positive vision."[viii]

-Dalai Lama

"Being available is the greatest gift anyone can give."

"You will never be better than *you* think you are."[ix]

- Bishop T. D. Jakes

"Finally, brothers, whatever is true, whatever is honorable, whatever is just, whatever is pure, whatever is lovely, whatever is commendable, if there is any excellence, if there is anything worthy of praise, think about these things."
-Philippians 4:8

<u>My two cents</u>: The bible says, "For as he thinks in his heart, so *is* he (NKJV)." I believe that, as well as the fact that if you concentrate on negative thoughts they will foster negative results. The same is true with positivity. We need to start dwelling on how things can change for the better, rather than harping on the negative experiences of our past. Things can only get better!

<u>Notes</u>:

_____
_____
_____

"When others are looking for an excuse to cry, find a reason to smile."

"The smile you put on someone's face costs you nothing, but it is priceless."

"In life, have a friend that is like a mirror and a shadow; a mirror doesn't lie and a shadow never leaves. "
-Shoulanda Copeland

"It takes more muscles to frown than it does to smile."

"Little children, let us not love in word or talk but in deed and in truth."
-1 John 3:18

My two cents: There are a lot of people that claim to be happy, but they are miserable on the inside. If we truly love our neighbors, as God's word says we should, we should take the time to see if the ones we care for are really telling us the truth by their actions. Pay attention to the signs.

Notes:
_____
_____
_____

"When it comes to those you love, sacrifice is evident."

"Friends show their love in times of trouble, not in happiness."[x]

"True friendship is like a rainbow. It is made of several different elements and shines through when the downpour stops."

"Two are better than one, because they have a good reward for their toil. For if they fall one will lift up his fellow. But woe to him who is alone when he falls and has not another to lift him up! Again, if two lie together, they keep warn, but how can one keep warm alone? And though a man might prevail against one who is alone, two will withstand him- a threefold cord is not quickly broken."
-Ecclesiastes 4:9-12

My two cents*:* Nowadays, it seems harder and harder to find *true* friends. Everyone seems to be out for self. If you find a *real* friend, hold on to them. For the value of friendship is limitless.

Notes:
_____
_____
_____

"Similar to a job interview or a first date, without positivity you are bound to never get what we want."

"Yesterday is not ours to recover, but tomorrow is ours to win or lose."[xi]

-Lyndon B. Johnson

"Keep your face to the sunshine and you cannot see a shadow."[xii]

-Helen Keller

"In God you will discover true happiness. When you lie to yourself and think that other things will satisfy you, who are you really attempting to deceive…"

"How can you find happiness if you keep settling for sorrow. Seek what you want in life and you will eventually discover it."

"Until now you have asked nothing in my name. Ask, and you will receive, that your joy may be full."

-John 16:24

My two cents: The choice to be happy starts with you. A wise person said that if you say you are going to have a good day or you are going to have a bad day, both statements are correct. The difference is which one you plan to make a reality.

Notes:
_____
_____
_____

"If you do what is easy, your life will be hard. But, if you do what is hard, your life will be easy."[xiii]
                    -Les Brown

"Life is slippery, here take my hand."[xiv]
                    -H. Jackson Brown, Jr.

"Let us never know what old age is. Let us know the happiness time brings, not count the years."[xv]
                    -Ausonius

"I would rather be happy in a shack next to those I love, rather than in a mansion all by myself."

"Beloved, let us love one another, for love is from God, and whoever loves has been born of God and knows God."
                    -1 John 4:7

My two cents: Life is not designed to be flawless and without bad times. But, keep in mind that those bad times make us appreciate the good times. Think about it. The memories of the good times are usually better than when we are actually experiencing them. Life is a precious gift. Be thankful.

Notes:
_____
_____
_____

"When I was 5 years old, my mother always told me that happiness was the key to life. When I went to school, they asked me what I wanted to be when I grew up. I wrote down 'happy.' They told me I didn't understand the assignment, and I told them they didn't understand life."[xvi]

-John Lennon

"When I was 6 years old, they tried to teach me man came from an ape, but I knew God created man! So, I would say they didn't understand life either."

-Debbie Garvy

"But the fruit of the Spirit is love, joy, peace, patience, kindness, goodness, faithfulness, gentleness, self-control; against such things there is no law."

-Galatians 5:22-23

<u>*My two cents*</u>: People will tell you what they think their version of happiness is all of your life, but it is your choice to believe what you see and hear from others and make your own decisions. To truly judge how happy someone is, look at the people they impact. Positivity attracts more positivity.

Notes:
_____
_____
_____

Chapter 2
Perseverance & Togetherness

"Where there is a will, and where there is faith, there is always a way."

"The number one difference between winners and losers, no matter how tall you are, old or young, gifted intelligently, or not is their attitude."

"The only reason why the lion is the king of the jungle is because of its attitude. If the lion has the attitude of a winner, it will eat. But, if it has the attitude of a loser it will be knocked off of it's thrown by an animal that may not even eat meat!"

"But as servants of God we commend ourselves in every way: by great endurance, in afflictions, hardships, calamities."
-2 Corinthians 6:4

My two cents: Fight as if your life depended on it, because it does. When you give up, you hardly realize how many other people that impacts. Now, your spouse sees failure as acceptable, as do your children. But, when you succeed, you will know that your impact is great, even if just one person is impacted.

Notes:
_____
_____
_____

"Change is the law of life. And those who look only to the past or present are certain to miss the future. [xvii]
-John F. Kennedy

"When you reach goal #1, set goal #2. Because if you get too comfortable, you might find yourself reaching for #1 again."

"Try using big words today in conversation, like *I CAN and IT'S POSSIBLE*. **Note the reactions by other people that normally think you don't try that hard at all."**

"Blessed is the man who remains steadfast under trial, for when he has stood the test he will receive the crown of life, which God has promised to those who love Him."
-James 1:12

<u>My two cents</u>: If you are not moving forward, you are comfortable. If you are comfortable you are moving backwards, because even when you're not learning you could be teaching the next generation the lessons that you have learned to become better. Each one, teach one.

<u>Notes</u>:
_____
_____
_____

"The greatest danger for most of us is not that our aim is too high and we miss, but that it is to low and we reach it."
-Michelangelo

"We must believe that we are gifted for something, and that this thing, at whatever cost, must be attained."[xviii]
-Marie Curie

"Those who fail to plan, plan to fail."

"…we rejoice in our sufferings, knowing that suffering produces endurance, and endurance produces character, and character produces hope, and hope does not put us to shame, because God's love has been poured into our hearts through the Holy Spirit who has been given to us."
-Romans 5:3-5

<u>*My two cents*</u>: We have to be thankful for the lessons we learn even in our trials, because that is what makes us who we are. Had we not have failed, we might not have valued the lessons we learned along the journey.

Notes:
_____
_____
_____

"Be careful who you listen to. It's usually your friends and family who are constantly talking you out of your dreams. People that don't have goals are slowly talking you out of yours. Be careful who and what you believe."[xix]

-Anonymous

"The price of success is hard work, dedication to the job at hand, and the determination that whether we win or lose, we have applied the best of ourselves to the task at hand."[xx]

-Vince Lombardi

"There is nothing greater than a team with a purpose and a determinant attitude."

"If you want to go fast, go alone. If you want to go far, do it together."[xxi]

-African Proverb

"For you have need of endurance, so that when you have done the will of God you may receive what is promised."
-Hebrews 10:36

My two cents: Sometimes its right when you feel like giving up is when deliverance comes. If you stick it out during the rough times you can rejoice when the blessings come.

Notes:
_____
_____
_____

"If you look for a problem and you look for a solution, you will likely find both. The question is which one are you focused on?"

"The biggest enemy of life is waste. What are you wasting your life on?"

"Are you willing to pay the cost of what it takes to reach your dreams, or are you settling for the discount price of staying where you are in life?"

"Count it all joy, my brothers, when you meet trials of various kinds, for you know that the testing of your faith produces steadfastness. And let steadfastness have its full effect, that you may be perfect and complete, lacking in nothing."
-James 1:2-4

My two cents: A wise person once said that success is not determined by doing what you desire perfectly at first, but by doing the what you yearn for in your heart, even if it means failing a few times along the way. Don't give up.

Notes:
_____
_____
_____

"What is worth having is worth working hard to obtain. If it's not worth it, your actions will prove it one way or another."

"Value is determined by a certain level of sacrifice."[xxii]
-Bishop T. D. Jakes

"Without a struggle, there can be no progress."[xxiii]
-Frederick Douglass

"Trust in the Lord with all your heart, and do not lean on your own understanding. In all your ways acknowledge Him and He will make straight your paths."
-Proverbs 3:5-6

<u>*My two cents*</u>: We are working hard at something whether we realize it or not; either we are working hard at staying the same or we are working hard at growing to become a better version of ourselves. We have to choose the latter of the two options to reach our potential.

Notes:
_____
_____
_____

"Time is one of the greatest resources lost to our temporary desires that cost us more than we can afford. So, make the best out of what you have left."

"Like a flower pedal that is swept away by a small breeze, if you find yourself easily swayed, you probably never had much of a foundation to being with."

"Be strong and courageous. Do not fear or be in dread of them, for it is the Lord your God who goes with you. He will not leave you nor forsake you."
-Deuteronomy 31:6

My two cents: We cannot do everything in our strength. We need to lean on God instead of always trying to do things on our own and when we pray and say that we will leave it in God's hands, which is exactly what we need to do. But, most of us say we will trust God, and yet we attempt to fix our problems ourselves. There is a difference between having faith and giving up. Having Faith mean being patient.

Notes:
_____
_____
_____

"If you never face a problem, you will never tame the issue. Keep fighting."

"Plan your work and work your plan."

"If you love something, you can get through anything."
-Female pilot

"We can become the pilots of our own planes to happiness and success. But, a lot of people are afraid to even get in the pilot's seat for fear of crashing before ever even taking off."

"For the Lord your God is He who goes with you to fight for you against your enemies, to give you the victory."
-Deuteronomy 20:4

<u>*My two cents*</u>: Often times we are afraid of making decisions for multiple reasons. But, we have to remember that the goals we have can become a reality if we just take an ounce of faith and put in the work necessary to achieve them. Rome wasn't built in a day and no brick wall has even been built without first laying one brick at a time.

Notes:
_____
_____
_____

"Opportunity rarely knocks twice; be ready to serve and meet the challenge(s) of any and all opportunities."
-Rick Williams

"I would rather have a strong engine and rugged-looking body, rather than something pretty on the outside with no heart."
-Dylan Andersen

"A dream means nothing without faith, determination, and hard work."

"The soul of the sluggard craves and gets nothing, while the soul of the diligent is richly supplied."
-Proverbs 13:4

My two cents: It is hard to see the light at the end of the tunnel when you are starting on a project or reaching for your dreams. But, through the bumps in the roads you later realize how the initials struggles helped you become who you are today.

Notes:
___
___
___

"**Real friends are family members without a birth certificate that matches your last name.**"
-Inspired by Shoulanda Copeland

"**A friendship, like any other relationship is something that takes persistence to make work.**"

"**My best friend is the one who brings out the best in me.**"[xxiv]
-Henry Ford

"**No man is an island and this life does not belong to us. We are all here to serve others.**"
-Inspired by Todd Garland

"**Greater love has no one than this, that someone lay down his life for his friends.**"
-John 15:13

<u>My two cents</u>: Friendship can be hard at times and it can be stressful too. But, there is nothing like a friend that is there for you through thick and thin and with you in the best of times and the worst of times.

Notes:
_____
_____
_____

"Most of the important things in the world have been accomplished by people who have kept on trying when there seemed to be no hope at all."xxv
                    -Dale Carnegie

"If you want to catch something that is eternal, you need to stop chasing after things that are temporary."

"Winners win and loser lose. I can say it any better than that!"

"And let us not grow weary of doing good, for in due season we will reap, if we do not give up."
                    -Galatians 6:9

<u>*My two cents*</u>: In the words of Bishop T. D. Jakes, when you are exhausted, you cannot trust how you feel. But, nevertheless, doing the right thing, even when no one is watching, is still good. If you feel that it is right in your heart, continue what you are doing. It will all work out in the end. Have faith young grasshopper.

Notes:
_____
_____
_____

"When you take your eyes off of what is important and your focus shifts towards a distraction, that's when accidents and tragedy can happen. But, when your focus is on the right thing, and you are determined, you will always come out victorious."

"As seeds, we grow through life taking turns watering each other, we're shined on by the Son, and God gives the increase."

"And I tell you, ask, and it will be given to you; seek, and you will find; knock, and it will be opened to you. For everyone who asks receives, and the one who seeks finds, and to the one who knocks it will be opened."
-Luke 11:9-10

My two cents: I hate to say it, but we all make excuses as to why we can't do something until we see someone else with our same situation or even worse doing exactly what we claim isn't possible. Stop making excuses for why you can't do *it,* and prove to not only yourself, but the world that you can and will be done!

Notes:
_____
_____
_____

"Comfort is a beautiful place, but nothing ever grows there."[xxvi]
                                       -Anonymous

"If you really think about it, most of the things that come easy usually aren't good for you anyway."
                                       -Reuben Holliman

"In the end…we only regret the chances we didn't take, the relationships we were afraid to have, and the decisions we waited too long to make."[xxvii]
                                       -Lewis Carroll

"For the righteous falls seven times and rises again, but the wicked stumble in times of calamity."
                                       -Proverbs 24:16

<u>*My two cents*</u>: Any great leader will tell you that determination is not about always being the fastest; it is about persistence. In the words of Dr. Briccio Valdez, you are always learning as long as you're alive, and if you think you've done it all and learned it all, you have already given up on true growth.

Notes:
_____
_____
_____

"It is not what we do, but why we do it that determines the satisfaction we get out of our efforts."
-Cailin Callahan Bridges

"Sometimes God allows us to go through thing so we can grow through things."

"Do all things, without grumbling or questioning, that you may be blameless and innocent, children of God without blemish in the midst of a crooked and twisted generation, among whom you shine as lights in the world."
-Philippians 2:14-15

My two cents: In modern times, people act as if hard work is something of the past. People are always looking for the next *fix* to make getting what you want easier and faster. But, as the saying goes, some things just don't change. Results will <u>never</u> come without hard work initially from someone.

Notes:
_____
_____
_____

"Obstacles are things a person sees when he or she takes their eyes off of their goals."[xxviii]

-E. Joseph Cossman

"When obstacles arise, you change your direction to reach your goal; you do not change your decision to get there."

-Zig Ziglar

"Perseverance is the hard work you do after you get tired of doing the hard work you already did."[xxix]

-Newt Gingrich

"Therefore, brothers, be all the more diligent to make your calling and election sure, for if you practice these qualities you will never fall."

-2 Peter 1:10

My two cents: One constant complain that several people make it *I don't have time*. Here's the truth, we all have the same 24 hours in a day. The biggest difference is, some people value their time, while others are counting down the seconds until it ends.

Notes:
_____
_____
_____

"With everything you do, be consistent."
-Damon Sefa

"Remember to stay focused, because the streets aren't chasing the same things you're chasing."[xxx]
-Ray Lewis

"It does not matter how slowly you go as long as you do not stop."[xxxi]
-Confucius

"And I am sure of this, that he who began a good work in you will bring it to completion at the day of Jesus Christ."
-Philippians 1:6

<u>***My two cents***</u>: When you're reaching towards a goal, it almost seems like there are more reasons to stop than there are reasons to keep going. But, there is no greater feeling than when you are exhausted after struggling for so long and finally see the light at the end of the tunnel. Being persistent has its own set of consequences, and not everyone will understand your walk of faith. But, I am sure they will all desire to be a part of the victory.

Notes:
_____
_____
_____

"Life is 10% of what happens to you and 90% of how you respond to it."

"Through perseverance, many people get success out of what seemed destined to be certain failure."[xxxii]

-Benjamin Disraeli

"Whoever is slothful will not roast his game, but the diligent man will get precious wealth."
-Proverbs 12:27

My two cents: In Zachary Avery's article, *The 5 Tips to Get Through Anything*, he explains that when reaching for a goal we should 1) take baby steps towards our goal. 2) Don't believe everything you think. 3) Reframe (a psychology term that means to recreate your perception of reality into something positive. 4) Build a support system. 5) Remember to provide self-care to your goals. The diamond was once a lump of coal, but after years of being under immense pressure and heat, it turned into a precious jewel.[xxxiii]

Notes:
_____
_____
_____

"We will either find a way or make one."[xxxiv]
                            -Hannibal, Carthaginian General

"A winner is just a loser who tried one more time."[xxxv]
                            -George M. Moore, Jr.

"Never confuse a single loss with the final victory."[xxxvi]
                            -Inspired by F. Scott Fitzgerald

"We are afflicted in every way, but not crushed; perplexed, but not driven to despair; persecuted, but not forsaken; struck down, but not destroyed…"
-2 Corinthians 4:8-9

<u>My two cents</u>: Entrepreneur magazine suggests these rules to follow when trying to stay on track towards your dreams: **A)** Keep the big vision at the forefront **B)** Fuel your vision and be persistent **C)** Make a plan, however, be flexible **D)** Be creative, but do not reinvent the wheel **E)** Don't get burned out **F)** Leverage any and everything to get things done, i.e. doctor's appointments or waiting on the mechanic **G)** Don't lose your sense of humor.[xxxvii]

Notes:
_____
_____
_____

Chapter 3
Overcoming Fear

"In order for you to have something you've never had before, you are going to have to do something you've never done before."[xxxviii]
-Thomas Jefferson

"Don't give up before God shows up."
–Pastor John Hadley of Anchor Church

"If you can't fly, then run. If you can't run, then walk. If you can't walk, then crawl, but whatever you do, you have to keep moving forward.[xxxix]
-Reverend Dr. Martin Luther King, Jr.

"Have I not commanded you? Be strong and courageous. Do not be afraid; do not be discouraged, for the LORD your God will be with you wherever you go."
-Joshua 1:9

My two cents: Your fears are fed by your doubt and lack of faith. If you have more faith and believe that you are safe, you will have less to fear. Stop feeding your fears and they will die of starvation.

Notes:
_____
_____
_____

"Thinking will not overcome fear, but action will."[xl]
-W. Clement Stone

"If your fears don't scare you then they're not big enough!"[xli]
-Unknown

"I learned that courage was not the absence of fear, but the triumph over it. The brave man is not he who does not feel afraid, but he who conquers that fear."[xlii]
-Nelson Mandela

"There is no fear in love, but perfect love casts out fear. For fear has to do with punishment, and whoever fears has not been perfected in love."
-1 John 4:18

My two cents: Although the feeling of fear itself may be real, often times the things we fear may not be. So, rest in the reassurance that God has cured us of our fears and has replaced that feeling with a sense of security and love.

Notes:
_____
_____
_____

"There is nothing to fear, but fear itself."
-Winston Churchill

"Fear is not real. It is a product of thought you create. Do not misunderstand me. Danger is very real. But fear is a choice."[xliii]
-Will Smith

"Even though I walk through the valley of the shadow of the death, I will fear no evil, for you are with me; your rod and your staff, they comfort me."
-Psalm 23:4-6

My two cents: Having fear in your relationships, your workplace, your home, or even your mind can make you feel imprisoned in places that you should be comfortable. Stop letting those fears shackle you. Break free from those chains by changing the way you think about your situations. People can only imprison themselves if they accept the notion that they are not free.

Notes:
_____
_____
_____

"Inaction breeds doubt and fear. Action breeds confidence and courage. If you want to conquer fear, do not sit home and think about it. Go out and get busy."[xliv]
                        -Dale Carnegie

"Mistakes are always forgivable, if one has the courage to admit them."[xlv]
                        -Bruce Lee

"The fear of man lays a snar, but whoever trusts in the Lord is safe."
-Proverbs 29:25

<u>*My two cents*</u>: Ironically, the act of fearing something shows me two things: it shows me that there is both faith and terror in the practice of fear. Someone believes in something that may or may not exist and they are horrified by the fact that it could be there as well. But, my question is, is it scarier to have faith in something positive and it be false, or know something is true and neglect to act on it?

Notes:
_____
_____
_____

A Maryland business owner cashed in on the states' patrons fear of crossing the Chesapeake Bay Bridge, which is a massive 4.3 miles long.[xlvi] **So, after the Maryland Transportations Authority police deemed their efforts to transport anxious passengers across the bridge a 'time-consuming and non-effective use of its resources,' Kent Island Express came to the rescue. Charging customers $25 one-way to drive their own vehicles over the bridge, people like Alex Robinson, saw fit to help those in need, as gephyrophobia (otherwise known as the fear of bridges), can be considered a seroius condition. Some people** *own* **fear and others let it own them.**

(Image is not of Chesapeak Bay Bridge)

"The prudent sees danger and hides himself, but the simple go on and suffe for it."
-Proverbs 27:12

My two cents: Fear has a weird way of controlling us if we're not too careful. We have to remember that our fears are only as powerful as we allow them to be. In all reality, we fear something that has not happen and may never happen. Instead, use that energy to fuel your desires, not halt your dreams.

Notes:
_____
_____
_____

"To overcome a fear, here's all you have to do: realize the fear is there, and do the action you fear anyway."[xlvii]
-Peter McWilliams

"Fear not, for I am with you; be not dismayed, for I am your God; I will strengthen you, I will help you, I will uphold you with my righeous right hand."
-Isaiah 41:10

<u>*My two cents*</u>: Fear come in all shapes and sizes, from starting a new job, moving to a new area, investing in your dreams, and even being a first-time parent. But, where mistakes are made there are also opportunites for growth and developent. Don't be afraid of change; be afraid of the unwillingness to change. Don't just go through life; grow through life.

Notes:
_____
_____
_____

"Willpower is the key to success. Successful people strive no matter what they feel by applying their will to overcome apathy, doubt or fear."[xlviii]

-Dan Millman

"God doesn't make mistakes and has made each of us in His own image. God is simply love. There should be no fear in love."[xlix]

-Martin O'Malley

"I sought the Lord, and he answered me; he delivered me from all of my fears."
-Psalm 34:4

<u>*My two cents*</u>: Althought the journey may seem impossible, that does not mean it will always be this way. It is all about persistence, faith, and persespective. Do not attempt to do all things in your own strength and wisdom. Do those things in Christ Jesus. Remember, the very word 'impossible' says I'm-possible. He gives you strength and gives you the glory.

<u>Notes</u>:
_____
_____
_____

"By replacing fear of the unknown with curiosity we open ourselves up to an infinite stream of possibility. We can let fear rule our lives or we can become childlike with curiosity, pushing our boundaries, leaping out of our comfort zones, and accepting what life puts before us."[1]
-Alan Watts

"When you overcome fear, you take what scares you, ingest it, and use it to fuel you forward. Strong people aren't people who are never afraid. But, they are people that do not let being scared stop them."
-Inspired by Todd Garland

"Behold, God is my salvation; I will trust, and will not be afraid; for the Lord God is my strength and my song, and he has become my salvation."
-Isaiah 12:2

<u>*My two cents*</u>: Fear comes from a lack of trust. So, we must trust and truly believe that things are going to be okay. Love the journey and be anxious for the process. When you rest in the comfort that you will be okay, you will start to look forward to the challenges of life, instead of dreading them.

Notes:
_____
_____
_____

"Courage is knowing what <u>not</u> to fear."[li]
                                        -Plato

"We all face adversity at some point in our lives, but the difference between winners and losers is that some people are still standing at the wall where they decided to stop and others have climbed over it one step at a time."

"For God gave us a spirit not of fear but of power and love and self-control."
                                        -2 Timothy 1:7

"When I am afriad, I put my trust in you."
-Psalm 56:3

My two cents: We all have to weather different storms. But, this does not mean that because someone else has not experienced the same trials we have gone through that they did not face difficulties. We all have the power to accept defeat or to rise to the occasion and press on.

Notes:
_____
_____
_____

"A prison is a place where you are incarated by others. Fear is a cell where you imprison yourself."

"Though an army encamp against me, my heart shall not fear; though war arise against me, yet I will be confident."
-Psalm 27:3

"Therefore, if anyone is in Christ, he is a new creation. The old has passed away; behold, the new has come."
-2 Corinthians 5:17

My two cents: I love the presence that some older people have, because they know who they are. They are not tempted by the same old things that used to tempt them. They speak their minds and they're not afraid to speak up against something they don't believe or agree with. They have the confidence and assurance to be themselves. We need to know who we are deep inside. We don't need to grow old to have this confidence and strength.

Notes:
_____
_____
_____

"Some days, 24 hours is too much to stay put in, so I take the day hour by hour, moment by moment. I break the task, the challenge, the fear into small, bite-size pieces. I can handle a piece of fear, depression, anger, pain, sadness, loneliness, illness. I actually put my hands up to my face, one next to each eye, like blinders on a horse."[lii]

-Regina Brett

"Beloved, do not believe every spirit, but test the spirits to see whether they are from God, for many false prophets have gone out into the world."

-1 John 4:1

"But to all who did receive him, who believed in his name, he gave the right to become children of God."
-John 1:12

<u>*My two cents*</u>: Ironically, we lose that sense of hope and imagination at some point throughout our lives. But, the question remains…why do we follow the crowd? Are they headed where you want to go? Just because those around us have stopped wanting more out of life does not mean that we should give up to. Go for your goals. You only live once!

Notes:
_____
_____
_____

"Fear of the unknown. They are afraid of new ideas. They are loaded with prejudices, not based upon anything in reality, but based on… if something is new, I reject it imediately because it's frightening to me. What they do instead is just stay with the familiar. You know, to me, the most beautiful things in all the universe, are the most mysterious."[liii]

-Wayne Dyer

"Courage is resistance to fear, mastery of fear, not absence of fear."

-Mark Twain

"If fear is strong enough to stop you, then your level of desire was weak from the beginning."

"Rejoice in the Lord always; again I will say, rejoice."
-Philippians 4:4

<u>*My two cents*</u>: We claim that we want to be happy, but we let our fears overshadow our dreams. We claim that we want to learn more about God, but we give in to our temptations more often that we give of our time to read the Word. We have to refocus the true benefactor of our joy, God.

Notes:
_____
_____
_____

"It is useless to fear not being accepted because people don't like you for who you are. If you look closely, you may realize that they don't like themselves so much; hence the reason they are trying to be like everyone else. Be happy in your own skin."

"For it is by grace you have been saved, through faith- and this is not from yourselves, it is the gift of God."
-Ephesians 2:8

My two cents: With plastic surgery being at an all-time high throughout worldwide, more people, male and female, are being dooped into believing that their image should conform to society's standards. My suggestion is, be happy with who you are. You will **never** keep up with the trends. And if you accept the lies, your happiness will depend on someone else's opinion of you, and you'll find yourself in a race you will never win.

Notes:
_____
_____
_____

"One of the greatest discoveries a man makes, one of his great surprises, is to find he/she can do what they were afraid they couldn't do."[liv]

-Henry Ford

"The Lord is my light and my salvation; whom shall I fear? The Lord is the stronghold of my life; of whom shall I be afraid?"
-Psalm 27:1

My two cents: We all have fears, especially when it comes to performing in front of others. But, where I believe we lose our focus is when we start to compare ourselves to others and base our growth upon that. We might not always be more talented than others, but we may have more heart. **Aim for being a better you and your fear of failure may start to dissolve into a passion for forming a better version of yourself for tomorrow.**

Notes:
_____
_____
_____

"For nothing will be impossible with God."
                                                    -Luke 1:37

"Fear is the path to the dark side. Fear leads to anger. Anger leads to hate. Hate leads to suffering."[lv]
                                                    -George Lucas

"For the law of the Spirit of life has set you free in Christ Jesus from the law of sin and death."
                                                    -Romans 8:2

<u>*My two cents*</u>: When dealing with trials in life, i.e. addiction, strife, health problems, depression, and anxiety, try not to always solve those problems yourself. Put those problems on God's shoulders and let Him lift you up in His strength. Remember, He already knows what you're struggling with.

Notes:
_____
_____
_____

"Fear of failure and fear of the unkown are always defeated by faith. Having faith in yourself, in the process of change, and in the new direction that change sets will reveal your own inner core of steel."[lvi]

-Georgette Mosbacher

"Just because you made a mistake, doesn't mean you are a mistake."[lvii]

-Georgette Mosbacher

"I cannot give you the formula for success, but I can give you the formula for failure- which is: Try to please everybody."[lviii]

-Herbert Bayard Swope

"Be strong, and let your heart take courage, all ou who wait for the Lord!"
-Psalm 31:24

My two cents: The fight inside of you should never stop until the entire fight is over, not when you start getting tired. Strength and endurance come together when your will becomes greater than your phsyical ability has been in the past. Make new goals and set new heights.

Notes:
___
___
___

Chapter 4
Strength

"People that wait on external circumstances to make internal changes will always find themselves coming up short."[lix]
-Inspired by Zig Ziglar

"Stay true to who you are, not who they claim you to be."

"I refuse to be a slave to who you think I am."[lx]
-Bishop T. D. Jakes

"The Lord is good, a stronghold in the day of trouble; he knows those who take refuge in him."
-Nahum 1:7

My two cents: Strength comes from enduring many pangs along our journey. Muscles do not get formed from a lack of effort. Wisdom does not come from a lack of trying new things. We must all grow through our mistakes. Through the pain, we become strong.

Notes:
_____
_____
_____

"My biggest problem and my biggest solution are found in the same place…me."
                                               -Anonymous

"Don't be so focused on the possession of something that you miss out on the mission."[lxi]
                                               -T. D. Jakes

"The LORD will fulfill his purpose for me; your steadfast love, O LORD, endures forever. Do not forsake the work of your hands."
-Psalm 138:8

<u>My two cents</u>: As a symbol of strength, constructing a plan to success is vital. Without a sense of purpose, it is almost impossible to achieve any goal. In order to have a purpose, you must know what your talent is. What are you really good at and how can you help yourself and others with this ability?

Notes:
_____
_____
_____

"Confidence is silent. Insecurities are loud."
                              -Lisa Toor

"If you do what is easy, your life will be hard. If you do what is hard, your life will be easy."[lxii]
                              -Les Brown

"We see our battles as occasions to see victory, not defeat!"
              -Pastor David Rogers of Crosspointe Church

"...And do not be grieved, for the joy of the Lord is your strength."
              -Nehemiah 8:10

<u>*My two cents*</u>: When it comes to people putting you down for whatever reason, you have to change your focus. What they say about you isn't a reflection of who you are; it is merely a reflection of how they perceive you. But, perception and reality are two different words for a reason.

Notes:
_____
_____
_____

"Whatever good things we build, end up building us."[lxiii]
-Jim Rohn

"I prefer to be true to myself, even at the hazard of incurring the ridicule of others, rather than to be false, and to incur my own abhorrence."
-Frederick Douglass

"And we know that for those who love God all things work together for good, for those who are called according to his purpose."
-Romans 8:28

My two cents: If a person considers you less than perfect, why would they settle for someone like you unless they considered themselves imperfect also? We are all judged daily, but where we make the mistake is putting too much effort into being liked. Instead, we should aim at being the best versions of ourselves that we can be, and trust that people will eventually catch up, and if not, it's their loss.

Notes:
_____
_____
_____

"Maturity is the ability to think, speak and act your feelings within the bounds of dignity. The measure of your maturity is how spiritual you become during the midst of your frustrations."[lxiv]

-Samuel Ullman

"Sometimes you might want to cry and give up, and that's okay. But after the tears have flowed and the sobs have passed, it's time to get through it."[lxv]

-Inspired by Eric Thomas

"The Lord is on my side; I will not fear. What can man do to me?"
-Psalm 118:6

My two cents: It may be difficult when you look around and see more reasons to be sad and carry sorrow in your hearts than happiness. But, hope can be found when you dare to seek it. Once we give up, only then will it stay hidden. We have to keep going. If there is one thing that I have learned it's that when we give up that is usually when God shows up. But, if we close ourselves off to even him, we will stay blind forever.

Notes:
_____
_____
_____

"Sorrow only conquered the people that never took its power back."

"Every great dream beings with a dreamer. Always remember, you have within you the strength, the patience, and the passion to reach for the stars to change the world.[lxvi]
                            -Harriet Tubman

"A hero is an ordinary individual who finds the strength to persevere and endure in spite of overwhelming obstacles."[lxvii]
                            -Christopher Reeve

"Though he fall, he shall not be cast headlong, for
the LORD upholds his hand."
-Psalm 37:24

<u>*My two cents*</u>: One crucial notion to remember is that as a parent, manager, authoritative figure, or individual you must be aware of the fact that more people are watching you than you may realize. They are watching everything you do. So, watch what you say and show others about the *real* you, not the version of you that you like to show off.

Notes:
_____
_____
_____

DON'T QUIT
By: Anonymous

When things go wrong as they sometimes will,
When the road you're trudging seems all up hill,
When the funds are low and the debts are high
And you want to smile, but you have to sigh,
When care is pressing you down a bit,
Rest if you must, but don't you quit.
Life is strange with its twists and turns
As every one of us sometimes learns
And many a failure comes about
When he might have won had he stuck it out;
Don't give up though the pace seems slow—
You may succeed with another blow.
Success is failure turned inside out—
The silver tint of the clouds of doubt,
And you never can tell just how close you are,
It may be near when it seems so far;
So stick to the fight when you're hardest hit—
It's when things seem worst that you must not quit.[lxviii]

"My flesh and heart may fail, but God is the strength of my heart and my portion forever."
-Psalm 73:26

<u>*My two cents*</u>: This was a poem I had to recite when I was a child, and it has always stuck with me. I find it amazing the excuses we will come up with when we no longer wish to pursue something. Whether it be an event or even a relationship, we essentially lessen its value with our words and negative thinking. But, honesty, hard work, and persistence are the keys to opening the door of success, no matter the size.

Notes:
_____
_____
_____

Strength in Self-Discipline

"But I say, walk by the Spirit, and you will not gratify the desires of the flesh."
-Galatians 5:16

"No man knows how bad he is till he has tried very hard to be good...Only those who try to resist temptation know how strong it is."[lxix]
-C. S. Lewis

"For because he himself has suffered when tempted, he is able to help those who are being tempted."
-Hebrews 2:18

"Flee from sexual immorality. Every other sin a person commits is outside the body, but the sexually immoral person sins against his own body. Or do you not know that your body is a temple of the Holy Spirit within you, whom you have from God? You are not your own, for you were bought with a price. So glorify God in your body."
-1 Corinthians 6:18-20

<u>***My two cents***</u>: Resisting the sins of the flesh, to me, is one of the hardest sins to overcome. However, these urges must be tamed and done so daily, sometimes hourly. But, most importantly, we must realize that our bodies are temples of God, not to be used to fulfill our own selfish desires. The temporary satisfaction isn't worth the shame of knowingly doing wrong.

Notes:
_____
_____
_____

"So whoever knows the right thing to do and fails to do it, for him it is sin."

-James 4:17

"If we confess our sins, he is faithful and just to forgive us our sins and to cleanse us from all unrighteousness."

-1 John 1:9

"I have stored up your word in my heart, that I might not sin against you."
-Psalm 119:11

My two cents: Having strength does not always mean doing things on your own. In fact, it takes a strong person to realize when they cannot complete a task or fix a situation by him or herself. However, we are not always brave enough to admit that our sinful ways are easier to succumb to then putting aside our egos and asking God to be our muscle. Let Him in! He can help…I promise!

Notes:
_____
_____
_____

"Gluttony is an emotional escape, a sign something is eating us."[lxx]

-Peter De Vries

"In general, mankind, since the improvement of cookery, eats twice as much as nature requires. Should we not show restraint and not stuff ourselves until we tire."[lxxi]

-Inspired by Benjamin Franklin

"Let no one say when he is tempted, "I am being tempted by God," for God cannot be tempted with evil, and he himself tempts no one. But each person is tempted when he is lured and enticed by his own desire."

-James 1:13-14

My two cents: Self-discipline is a tough issue to handle regarding any of the basic human desires, gluttony, sexual immorality, covetousness, etc. However, when we give in to our desires without restraint, we are not even making an attempt to better ourselves. This is not a full attempt at getting closer to the Lord. Maya Angelou said it best. *When you know better, you do better*.

Notes:
_____
_____
_____

"God grant me the serenity to accept the things I cannot change; courage to change the things I can, and wisdom to know the difference."[lxxii]

-Reinhold Niebuhr

"Consider the postage stamp: its usefulness consists in the ability to stick to one thing till it gets there."[lxxiii]

-Josh Billings

"Guard well your spare moments. They are like uncut diamonds. Discard them and their value will never be known. Improve them and they will become the brightest gems in a useful life."[lxxiv]

-Ralph Waldo Emerson

"For we do not have a high priest who is unable to sympathize with our weaknesses, but one who in every respect has been tempted as we are, yet without sin."
-Hebrews 4:15

<u>*My two cents*</u>: Be strong and confident in who you are saved by, not just be who you are. Remember, none of us deserve the grace we receive daily. Be confident, but be humble.

<u>Notes</u>:
_____
_____
_____

Strength- having a purpose

"Just because you cannot see the destination at the end of the road, that does not mean that you are not destined to take that turn and proceed. Keep moving forward."

"Never give up on something you can't go a day without thinking about."
-Shoulanda Copeland

"Great minds have purposes; others have wishes[lxxv]."
-Washington Irving

"Declaring the end from the beginning and from ancient times things not yet done, saying, 'My counsel shall stand, and I will accomplish all my purpose…"
-Isaiah 46:10

<u>My two cents</u>: Are you on target, or are you aimlessly drudging through life? Have you figured out what your purpose is or have you ever even dared to ask the question? Work on your goals and dreams, but remember that you are not working towards them alone. In order for them to work, you must first have faith that they will.

Notes:
_____
_____
_____

Chapter 5
What Does Love Look Like?

"Love is not just something you say, it's something you show."

"A loved one does for another without being told, but they also do what they are told with love."

"God loves you as though you are the only person in the world, and He loves everyone the way He loves you."[lxxvi]
-Dr. David Jeremiah

"But for those who hope in the Lord will renew their strength. They will soar on wings like eagles; they will run and not grow weary, they will walk and not be faint."
-Isaiah 40:31

My two cents: True love has no bounds and soars unconditionally. It is tested and it persistent. And the love that we share is not of our own; it is from God who first loved us. Sometimes, it is difficult to love the *unlovable*. But, that doesn't mean that it is impossible and not necessary.

Notes:
_____
_____
_____

"Let love be genuine. Abhor what is evil; hold fast to what is good. Love one another with brotherly affection. Outdo one another in showing honor. Do not be slothful in zeal, be fervent in spirit, serve the Lord. Rejoice in hope, be patient in tribulation, be constant in prayer. Contribute to the needs of the saints and seek to show hospitality."

-Romans 12:9-13

"Courtesy is the simplest act of love."

-Dr. David Jeremiah

"Let all that you do be done in love."
-1 Corinthians 16:14

My two cents: So often, we find ourselves looking for the faults in people. But, we seldom seek the strengths in a person. My mentor, Minister Ron Jackson, says that although we all fall short of the glory of God, we should focus on the positive characteristics of people. When we hone in on the positive, we get to enjoy them more for who they are and who they want to be, not just their imperfections.

Notes:
_____
_____
_____

"Love what has been given to you. Do not lust after what has been given to someone else. That is not your prize."

"And lead us not into temptation, but deliver us from evil."
-Matthew 6:13

"And he said to them, "Take care, and be on your guard against all covetousness, for one's life does not consist in the abundance of his possessions."
-Luke 12:15

The neighbor's house   Your house

"You shall not covet your neighbor's house; you shall not covet your neighbor's wife, or his male servant, or his female servant, or his ox, or his donkey, or anything that is your neighbor's."
-Exodus 20:17

<u>*My two cents*</u>: Be careful what you fall in love with. Some people fall in love with having money, others love cars, jewelry, sleep, food, and other meaningless, yet temporary things. Mainly, there are a great deal of us who love what others have. The lust for the possessions of others is covetousness, i.e. their house, cars, financial situation, wife, or husband. Do not yearn after what someone else has. It does not belong to you. Period.

Notes:
_____
_____
_____

"But sexual immorality and all impurity or covetousness must not even be named among you, as is proper among saints."
-Ephesians 5:3

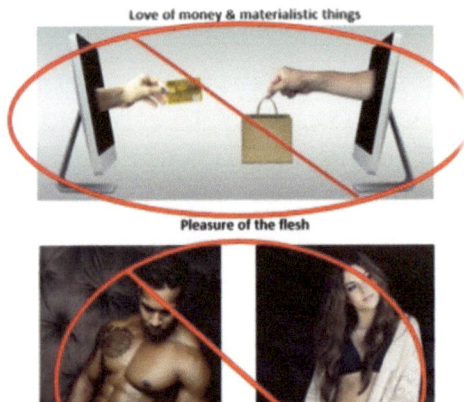

"Owe no one anything, except to love each other, for the one who loves another has fulfilled the law. For the commandments, "You shall not commit adultery, You shall not murder, You shall not steal, You shall not covet," and any other commandment, are summed up in this word: "You shall love your neighbor as yourself." Love does no wrong to a neighbor; therefore love is the fulfilling of the law."
-Romans 13:8-10

<u>*My two cents*</u>: Frequently people lust after the wrong things and the wrong people. This can lead to many painful consequences. Being in love with your image can be costly, and I don't just mean in money. As a husband or a wife, remember that there's no such thing as *your* money anymore. When you selfishly feed into your addiction to acquire more things you don't need, you're now stealing from your family.

Notes:
_____
_____
_____

"The best way to teach someone how to love is to show them how to be loved."[lxxvii]

-Inspired by Zig Ziglar

"Always, always, always look for the good in people."

-Inspired by Minister Ron Jackson, Sr.

"Let all that you do be done in love."

-1 Corinthians 6:14

"Listening and giving of your time are two of the best gifts you can give, and no one loves anything better than being asked about themselves."

-Rick Williams

"We love because he first loved us."
-1 John 4:19

<u>*My two cents*</u>: In the words of one of my mentors growing up, Rick Williams, he says that in order for a person to know that you truly love them, you spell that out to them. True love is spelled T.I.M.E., not L.O.V.E. **You can't just say you love people; you have to show your love to people**. Words only go so far when your actions show that you may just like them, versus 'I absolutely love you.'

<u>Notes</u>:
_____
_____
_____

"When you love, you don't have to chase love or fear it's going unanswered. When you love, it will fill you up, fill others up, and spill over into every area of your life."[lxxviii]
-Jon Gordon

"If he/she's amazing, they won't be easy. If they're easy, they won't be amazing. If they're worth it, you won't give up. If you give up, you're not worthy. ... Truth is, everybody is going to hurt you; you just got to find the ones worth suffering for."[lxxix]
-Bob Marley

"For you were called to freedom, brothers. Only do not use your freedom as an opportunity for the flesh, but through love serve one another."
-Galatians 5:13

My two cents: Love what you have in front of you. Try to appreciate the people in your life right now. If you are smart, you might realize that today is a gift; that's why they call it the present.

Notes:
_____
_____
_____

"Love is unconditional. That means that no matter what you will be there, do anything, sacrifice your wants, and remain constant, even when you don't feel like it."

"When you trip over love, it is easy to get up. But when you fall in love, it is impossible to stand again."[lxxx]
-Albert Einstein

"God proved His love on the Cross. When Christ hung, and bled, and died, it was God saying to the world, 'I love you'."[lxxxi]
-Billy Graham

"Beloved, if God so loved us, we also out to love one another."
-1 John 4:11

My two cents: It is so easy to find faults in one another, but, how much effort does it take to do that. Now, with the right focus in mind, how much effort does it take to show true love? My question is, if you know the reward, why are we still fighting backwards finding mistakes in those we claim that we would do anything for?

Notes:
_____
_____
_____

"I love you without knowing how, or when, or from where. I love you simply, without problems or pride: I love you in this way because I do not know any other way of loving but this, in which there is no I or you, so intimate that your hand upon my chest is my hand, so intimate that when I fall asleep your eyes close."[lxxxii]

-Pablo Neruda

"Sometimes a gaze and a smile can show love better than words can describe."

"I am unworthy of all your gracious love, your faithfulness, and everything that you've done for your servant."
-Genesis 32:10

My two cents: Love shows a sacrifice in our normal routines. Love will make you divert your attention for something less important. It may also allow you to see and experience many great times. But, most of all, the vitally important thing about love is that you give it no matter what, even if you're not getting it in return; love anyway.

Notes:
_____
_____
_____

When Loving is Hard

"For if you love those who love you, what reward have you? Do not even the tax collectors do the same?"
                                                    -Matthew 5:46

"I believe that imagination is stronger than knowledge. That myth is more potent than history. That dreams are more powerful than facts. That hope always triumphs over experience. That laughter is the only cure for grief. And I believe that love is stronger than death."
                                                    -Robert Fulghum

"A new command I give you: Love one another. As I have loved you, so you must love one another. By this all people will know that you are my disciples, if you have love for one another."
-John 13:34

My two cents: Sometimes those that are the hardest to love, need love the most. We have to learn to look passed our petty differences and show the love we expect to receive. Those that are young and are coming up behind us will look up to us and see how they should be, even when you think they're not watching.

Notes:
_____
_____
_____

"For God he so loved the world that he sent his only son, that whoever believes in him should not perish but have eternal life."

-John 3:16

"A woman's heart should be so hidden in God that a man has to seek Him just to find her."[lxxxiii]

-Max Lucado

"Life is short. Kiss slowly, laugh insanely, love truly and forgive quickly."[lxxxiv]

-Paulo Coelho

"Let the husband render to his wife the affection due her, and likewise also the wife to her husband."
-1 Corinthians 7:3

My two cents: Build a future, and in it include those you love and cherish and you will find peace. If you find sorrow, recognize that you might have left those same people out and never appreciated those who were for you all along.

Notes:
_____
_____
_____

"You don't really understand human nature, unless you know why a child on a marry-go-round waves at his parents every time around. Love is also the reason why the parents always wave back."
                              -Christina Hale

"Sometimes people put up walls, not to keep others out, but to see who cares enough to break them down."[lxxxv]
                              -Banana Yoshimoto

"Being deeply loved by someone gives you strength, while loving someone deeply gives you courage."[lxxxvi]
                              -Laozi

"Above all, keep loving one another earnestly, since love covers a multitude of sins."
-1 John 4:8

My two cents: Loving others is a selfless act that is intentional and purposeful. You cannot accidentally love someone. It is done with thought and consideration. <u>Love like you mean it!</u>

Notes:
_____
_____
_____

Sacrifice

"The most precious gift we can offer anyone is our attention. When mindfulness embraces those we love, they will bloom like flowers."[lxxxvii]

-Nhat Hanh

"Love sometimes requires us to go outside of our comfort zone and put someone else's needs in front of our own. But, when that love is returned it can be more satisfying than any gift money can buy."

"The cost of our love can include all of our money, time, energy, effort, and care. But, the reward is simple; it's everything."

"So now faith, hope, and love abide, these three; but the greatest of these is love."
-1 Corinthians 13:13

My two cents: The love for something you need, like a job or a reliable vehicle is the love of necessity. But, the love that you show a family member or a friend is a gift. This gift is eternal and cannot be replaced with material things. It comes directly from you and is exemplary of how God loves us.

Notes:
_____
_____
_____

"In tough times our job can be taken away, as well as our cars, our house, and even our money. But no collector can steal the love that's in your heart. For it is sacred, even in the walls of a prison."

"And as you wish that others would do to you, do so to them."
-Luke 6:31

Referring to the Ten Commandments: "The second is this: 'You shall love your neighbor as yourself.' There is no other commandment greater than these."
-Mark 12:31

"A friend loves at all times, and a brother is born for adversity."
-Proverbs 17:17

My two cents: A good friend may be found from time to time, but a great friend is as precious as a diamond. Love does not have boundaries. It is tested, shaken, and tried; yet it is not easily given up and is not quickly earned. It is a miracle that we even know what love is. Value who you have, for it may be too late to do so one day.

Notes:
_____
_____
_____

Chapter 6
Dealing with Pain

"The righteous cry out, and the Lord hears them; he delivers them from all their troubles."
-Psalm 34:17

"Don't be someone's down time, part time, or some time. If they can't be there for you all the time, maybe they're not worth your time.
-Shoulanda Copeland

"He will wipe away every tear from their eyes, and death shall be no more, neither shall there be mourning, nor crying, nor pain anymore, for the former things have passed away."
-Revelation 21:4

My two cents: Dealing with pain can feel agonizing, mainly because as the victim, you tend to keep replaying specific events in your mind to make sense of it all. But, stop allowing people that hurt you in your past to acquire rent in your thoughts. Evict them as soon as possible and let them go forever!

Notes:
_____
_____
_____

Secrets and gossip

"Never tell all of your secrets. Only speak about that which you don't mind being repeated. Always remember that everybody gossips."
-Robbie Cornelius

"The worst distance between two people is misunderstanding."
-Shoulanda Copeland

"Let no corrupting talk come out of your mouths, but only such as is good for building up, as fits the occasion, that it may give grace to those who hear."
-Ephesians 4:29

<u>*My two cents*</u>: When covering the topic of secrets and gossips, one has to think about the intention behind spreading a rumor or creating a secret in the first place. If the secret is meant to protect someone from information that could put others at risk, that's one thing. But, if words are spoken about someone without their knowledge or an opportunity to defend themselves, these things are not done in love, but in evil.

<u>Notes</u>:

_____

_____

_____

"Don't pay the price for who you used to be. Enjoy the reality of who you are becoming."
                              -Inspired by Zig Ziglar

"Just because someone left you in a position in your life making you feel like garbage that does not give you permission to own that title."

"I have said these things to you, that in me you may have peace. In the world you will have tribulation. But take heart; I have overcome the world."
-John 16:33

<u>*My two cents*</u>: One person's trash is another person's treasure. Just because one person might have not seen the value in you at the time, does not mean that you are unwanted. Another person may take the time to see what you're really worth, if that's the Lord's will for your life, and they will help brush off the blemishes and help you shine.

Notes:
_____
_____
_____

Fear of the dark
-Sri Chinmoy
"Listen to the inner light;
It will guide you.
Listen to the inner Peace;
It will feed you.
Listen to the inner Love;
It will transform you,
It will divinize you,
It will immortalize you."[lxxxviii]

"Again Jesus spoke to them saying, "I am the light of the world. Whoever follows me will not walk in darkness, but will have the light of life."
-John 1:5

My two cents: If you walked into a house and only one corner in one room was illuminated, could you really say that you have seen everything in that room? But, if the entire room was lit and you could see everything in the room, could you then say you've experienced what was in that room? Now, imagine if your life was the room…are you still experiencing life in the corner without the Lord as your light, or are you fully aware of what and who is present?

Notes:
_____
_____
_____

"Darkness cannot drive out darkness; only light can do that. Hate cannot drive out hate; only love can do that."[lxxxix]
-Rev. Dr. Martin Luther King, Jr.

"Hope is being able to see that there is light despite all of the darkness."[xc]
-Desmond Tutu

"I will love the light for it shows me the way, yet I will endure the darkness because it shows me the stars."
-Og Mandino

"But if we walk in the light, as he is in the light, we have fellowship with one another, and the blood of Jesus his Son cleanses us from all sin."
-1 John 1:7

<u>*My two cents*</u>: John 14:6 says that Jesus is the way, the truth, and the life. If he is the light of the world, would this not illuminate the path<u>way</u>, which would lead us to the true perfecter of our faith, whom gave us <u>life</u>?

Notes:
_____
_____
_____

Physical pain and spiritual pain

"For I consider that the sufferings of this present time are not worth comparing with the glory that is to be revealed to us."
-Romans 8:18

"I can do all things in Christ who strengthen me."
-Philippians 4:13

"God, who foresaw your tribulation, has specially armed you to go through it, not without pain but without stain."[xci]
-C. S. Lewis

"And whenever you stand praying, forgive, if you have anything against anyone, so that your Father also who is in heaven may forgive you your trespasses."
-Mark 11:25

My two cents: Pain has an interesting way of teaching us life lessons, such as childbirth and growing pains. We all take part in our fair share of pain and no one is exempt from it, no matter your age, ethnicity, financial status or class. We must also be grateful for what we have and learn to persevere so that we are not held hostage by the memories of past.

Notes:
_____
_____
_____

Overcoming Grief

"Grief is in two parts. The first is loss. The second is the remaking of life."[xcii]

-Anne Roiphe

"It takes strength to make your way through grief, to grab hold of life and let it pull you forward."[xciii]

-Patti Davis

"I will not say, do not weep, for not all tears are an evil."

-J. R. R. Tolkien

"Blessed are those who morn, for they shall be comforted."
-Matthew 5:4

My two cents: There are several elements of life that cause grief, including: decisions that cause regret, to the loss of a loved one, to failed relationships; the list is endless. But, we have the choice to build a house in the pit of despair, or we can move on and find happiness in the things we still have in front of us. Choose…

Notes:
_____
_____
_____

Grief Continued...

"You will lose someone you can't live without, and your heart will be badly broken, and the bad news is that you never completely get over the loss of your beloved. But this is also the good news. They live forever in your broken heart that doesn't seal back up. And you come through. It's like having a broken leg that never heals perfectly—that still hurts when the weather gets cold, but you learn to dance with the limp."
-Anne Lamott

"Therefore let those who suffer according to God's will entrust their souls to a faithful Creator while doing good."
-1 Peter 4:12-13

<u>*My two cents*</u>: An orphan may never be satisfied that they have no parents, until they are adopted and discovered that their biological parents were unfit to raise them. As they say, hindsight is 20/20; it takes wise eyes and an open mind to realize you might just be *exactly* where you are supposed to be in life. Sadly, most of us never realize how the dots are connected until much later.

Notes:
_____
_____
_____

Physical Pain

"Bad things do happen; how I respond to them defines my character and the quality of my life. I can choose to sit in perpetual sadness, immobilized by the gravity of my loss, or I can choose to rise from the pain and treasure the most precious gift I have- life itself."[xciv]
  -Walter Anderson

"Find a place inside where there's joy, and the joy will burn out the pain."
  -Joseph Campbell

"The Lord sustains him on his sickbed; in his illness you restore him to full health."
-Psalm 41:3

<u>*My two cents*</u>: In my life experience, I have discovered that physical pain has to do more with perception than the feeling. I used to think that pain was a consequence of God not loving me, but how can you be grateful for the good times if we never experience the bad times. Gratitude, like love must be consistent.

Notes:
_____
_____
_____

Physical Pain on the field

"There is no physical pain, no spiritual wound, no anguish of soul or heartache, no infirmity or weakness you or I ever confront in mortality that the Savior did not experience first. In a moment of weakness we may cry out, 'No one knows what it is like. No one understands.' But the Son of God perfectly knows and understands, for He has felt and borne our individual burdens."[xcv]

-David A. Bednar

"And after my skin has been destroyed, yet in my flesh I shall see God…"

-Job 19:26

"Count it all joy, my brothers, when you meet trials of various kinds, for you know that the testing of you faith produces steadfastness. And let steadfastness have its full effect, that you may be perfect and complete, lacking in nothing."
-James 1:2-4

<u>*My two cents*</u>: It is amazing that while we are enduring pain, specifically physical pain, it remains the only thing we think about. It is hard to look passed it or think of anything else more pressing but what is right in front of us. This, to me, shows us how vulnerable we really are. We all have limits. But, not God.

Notes:
_____
_____
_____

Pain on the battlefield

"Even today we raise our hand against our brother... We have perfected our weapons, our conscience has fallen asleep, and we have sharpened our ideas to justify ourselves as if it were normal we continue to sow destruction, pain, death. Violence and war lead only to death."
                                           -Pope Francis

"And you will hear of wars and rumors of wars. See that you are not alarmed, for this must take place, but the end is not yet."
                                           -Matthew 24:6

Beloved, do not be surprised at the fiery trial when it comes upon you to test you, as though something strange were happening to you."
-1 Peter 4:12

<u>*My two cents*</u>: It seems frustrating and confusing to have to bare being in pain, suffering, and weak without answers to some of the most agonizing questions that plague us. No matter how much we study, we will never know everything, and we are not meant to. We all experience pain and frustration at some time or another. We must learn how to embrace it and not let it stop us.

Notes:
_____
_____
_____

Chapter 7
Having Faith

"Never be afraid to trust an unknown future to a known God[xcvi]."

-Corrie Ten Boom

"God gives us what we have in freedom and in love. The devil deceives us into believing we can be our own Gods, inherently making us slaves to those very desires."

-Inspired by Dr. Charles Stanley

"And without faith it is impossible to please him, for whoever would draw near to God must believe that he exists and that he rewards those who seek him."

-Hebrews 11:6

"Now faith is the assurance of things hoped for, the conviction of things not seen."
-Hebrews 11:1

My two cents: It is hard to have faith at times, especially the bad times. But, we seldom bow on our knees in the good times. We should not be ashamed to worship the Lord and show our gratitude in good times or bad. Seek His face not just His hand.

Notes:
_____
_____
_____

"And Jesus answered them, "Have faith in God. Truly, I say to you, whoever says to this mountain, 'Be taken up and thrown into the sea,' and does not doubt in his heart, but believes that what he says will come to pass, it will be done for him."
-Mark 11:22-23

"But the one who endures to the end will be saved."
-Matthew 24:13

"Life is not meant to be easy; it is not a playground, it's a battlefield."
-Inspired by Pastor David Rogers

"If we endure, we will also reign with him; if we deny him, he also will deny us."
-2 Timothy 2:12

My two cents: When you are around others, what is usually the topic of discussion? We have the power to decide what is most pressing in our conversations, but how many of us choose to talk about things that are productive? Or, do we find ourselves engulfed by the constant barrage of destructive and meaningless matters? Be careful of what you become a part of.

Notes:
___
___
___

"There is no need for a temple for those who believe, because God and Jesus are our temple."

-Inspired by Revelation 21:22

"Sometimes God will bring us down to our knees, which ironically forces us to look up to Him."

"Just because you can't see the plan till the end does not mean it won't be carried out!"[xcvii]

-Inspired by Steve Harvey

"For we walk by faith, not by sight."
-2 Corinthians 5:7

My two cents: Far too often, we assume that our trials are meant to punish us. But, in my experience, I have discovered that our trials show us a glimpse of how we are really in God's grace. We think we are having rough times, until we see someone struggling far worse than we are and it puts things into perspective.

Notes:

_____
_____
_____

"In all your ways acknowledge him, and he will make straight your paths."
-Proverbs 3:6

Jesus said, "Whoever drinks the water I give the will never thirst."
-John 4:14

"If you truly have faith you don't say phrases like, "I can't." Real faith says, "I CAN" with a cross at the end."
-Nadean "Gwynn" Poole

"And whatever you ask in prayer, you will receive, if you have faith."
-Matthew 21:22

My two cents: This last quote by Jesus seems like a simple one, but how many of us hear the word of God and still question it? Sometimes we ask for a sign, get the sign, and because we do not see or hear what we want, we refuse the sign. We have to be obedient if we consider ourselves true followers of a might a righteous God.

Notes:
_____
_____
_____

"Some people only follow Jesus based out of obligation and they sin so often that they don't even feel conviction from the Holy Spirit. In doing so, are we really saved or are we just going through the motions?"

-Inspired by Pastor Dr. James McDonald

"If any of you lacks wisdom, let him ask God, who gives generously to all without reproach and it will be given him. But let him asking in faith, with no doubting, for the one who doubts is like a wave of the sea that is driven and tossed by the wind. For that person must not suppose that he will receive anything from the Lord; he is a double-minded man, unstable in all his ways."

-James 1:5-8

"Praying at all times in the Spirit, with all prayer and supplication. To that end keep alert with all perseverance, making supplication for all the saints."
-Ephesians 6:18

<u>*My two cents*</u>: the term 'supplication' means to ask or beg for something humbly. How often do we ask something of Him that will help someone else in need or to thank Him for what we already have? **<u>Praying should be done out of honor and love, not out of obligation or as a last resort</u>**.

Notes:
_____
_____
_____

"So do not be ashamed to testify about our Lord, or ashamed of me his prisoner. But join with me in suffering of the gospel, by the power of God, who has saved us and called us to a holy life- not because of his own purpose and grace."
-2 Timothy 1:8

"If the epicenter of our lives is out of focus then it can cause an earthquake in our foundation."

"I am coming soon. Hold fast what you have, so that no one may seize your crown."
-Revelation 3:11

My two cents: I believe that all too often through life we cherish the wrong things in our adolescence and even throughout adulthood. It is usually when we become older that we learn to cherish the things in life that are truly important, our family, close friends, and our relationship with God. It is then that we realize that we wasted so much time attempting to acquire stuff and hoped that people liked us that we have missed out on having a deeper relationship with someone that has been chasing us all of our lives.

Notes:
_____
_____
_____

"Turn your worry into worship and God will turn your burdens into blessings."
-Rabirah L. Thomas

"God did not put us on this earth to fail."

"Enjoy the moment you are in instead of only wishing for the future. *It* will get here when it is time. Enjoy right now. Look for and acknowledge all your blessings."
-Inspired by Monica Sue Drawyer

"Truly, Truly, I say to you, whoever believes has eternal life."
-John 6:47

My two cents: We sometimes forget that He has a higher purpose for us and although we may suffer temporarily, we are not meant to endure pain and strife forever. Often times when we look in the mirror, we think of how we can accomplish things on our own, but we have to remember that **He is working through us** and we are never truly alone.

Notes:
_____
_____
_____

"It takes very little effort to not believe in something. The refusal to try is guaranteed failure."

"Every closed door is not a missed opportunity, sometimes it's God's grace saving us from a mistake. When God is directing our path, He will close doors that no man can open, and He will open doors that no man can close. You can be sure that anything behind a door that God closed was going to open up problems that you didn't expect or want."
-Sylvester Nvwc

"He is my God and I trust Him."
-Psalm 91:2

My two cents: Seldom do we ever look at a situation that did not work out as a gift, until much later. Frequently, we do not credit a desire that did not work out as a benefit until we have something greater than what we thought we wanted, but is this realization not a lack of faith. We have to be faithful, even in what seems to be the bad times.

Notes:
_____
_____
_____

"When you are with your friends, do you rush to share with them your desire to acquire more things, or to share what's in your heart?"

"You cannot follow Jesus and play it safe."
-Pastor David Butler

"It seems like we do as little as possible, but have such high expectations for God."

"Humble yourselves, therefore, under the mighty hand of God so that at the proper time he may exalt you, casting all your anxieties on him, because he cares for you."
-1 Peter 5:6-7

My two cents: Although we might not realize it, we all bow down to something, whether it be our obligations, our spouses, our fears, our addictions, or our desires, we all fall victim to putting something ahead of our relationship with God at times. We have to remain humble and stay true to him.

Notes:
___
___
___

"Having faith is a choice made daily, and that applies to the future of any relationship. Where there is temptation to go outside of that relationship is a choice; one can either give in to that temptation or rise up."

"Never overestimate your enemy or underestimate your God."

"Trust God for the impossible-miracles are His department. Our job is to do our best, letting the Lord do the rest."[xcviii]
-Dr. David Jeremiah

"Be still, and know that I am God. I will be exalted among the nations, I will be exalted in the Earth."
-Psalm 46:10

<u>My two cents</u>: In reference to our goals, dreams, and aspirations, we tend to think that God has given up on us, or maybe we're not supposed to have what we want, or we feel as though we may not deserve what we are blessed to receive. But, we need to remember whose team we are on. We are already on the winning team.

Notes:
_____
_____
_____

"When it comes to people putting you down for whatever reason, you have to change your focus. What they say about you isn't a reflection of who you are; it is merely a reflection of how they perceive you. But, perception and reality are two different words for a reason."

"Admit it! We're ALL a mess. That's why we all need Jesus to clean us up."
                                        -Susan Fountain

"Study your bible, because Satan studies you."
                                        -Shoulanda Copeland

"You believe that God is one; you do well. Even the demons believe- and shudder!
-James 2:19

My two cents: There are several times throughout our lives that we find ourselves feeling like we are our own Gods. But, there are situations outside of our control and the questions remains, how do we console someone that is dealing with devastating news, like cancer? How do we calm someone with anxiety? That's God's job to be the individual that allows something to happen or alters the course of the event.

Notes:

"Anything that runs itself usually runs downhill."
  -Iris Exum

"Faith is not the belief that God will do what you want. It is the belief that God will do what is right."[xcix]
  -Max Lucado

"That your faith might not rest in the wisdom of men but in the power of God."
  -1 Corinthians 2:5

My two cents: Frequently, we find ourselves confused and even frustrated with the events of life. I believe that a huge reason why we find ourselves so miserable and upset is because we think we know best. But, what I mean to say is we think we know better than God. We think we deserve different lives, and by *different,* I mean better. Our ego causes us to be impatient and because of this, we fail to realize that God may be putting other things in place so that when we do get to that place in our lives, if that is His will, we will be mature enough to handle it.

Notes:
_____
_____
_____

Footprints in the sand
-Mary Stevenson (1936)

One night I dreamed a dream.
As I was walking along the beach with my Lord.
Across the dark sky flashed scenes from my life.
For each scene, I noticed two sets of footprints in the sand,
One belonging to me and one to my Lord.

After the last scene of my life flashed before me,
I looked back at the footprints in the sand.
I noticed that at many times along the path of my life,
especially at the very lowest and saddest times,
there was only one set of footprints.

This really troubled me, so I asked the Lord about it.
"Lord, you said once I decided to follow you,
You'd walk with me all the way.
But I noticed that during the saddest and most troublesome times of my life,
there was only one set of footprints.
I don't understand why, when I needed You the most, You would leave me."

He whispered, "My precious child, I love you and will never leave you
Never, ever, during your trials and testing's.
When you saw only one set of footprints,
It was then that I carried you."

My two cents: To me, it symbolizes the unconditional love that God has for us. There were many moments throughout my life where I felt like God had abandoned me and left me to fend for myself, but I've realized that He has a plan for those who believes.

Notes:
_____
_____
_____

"Many of us are seeking a blessing from God, but are simultaneously trying to go around him like a person trying to get into a locked house through the window or the chimney. Faith is the doorway to our salvation, but some of us are failing to see <u>who</u> the key is."

"You know what fear and faith have I common? They both believe in a future that hasn't happened yet."[c]
-Jon Gordon

"Even an atheist's favorite subject is God."
-Inspired by Eddie Williams

"Whoever is not with me is against me, and whoever does not gather with me scatters."
-Matthew 12:30

<u>*My two cents*</u>: One key lesson that I have learned is that although we believe we have all of the keys to make life perfect, we are so unprepared, nor are we qualified. Our credentials are lacking in the department of being able to resolve every problem that exists, including our own. So, we have to learn to use the correct tools, and lean on His understanding.

Notes:
_____
_____
_____

"When people let you down, God will lift you up….if you believe in Him."
                                    -Inspired by Javi Leo

"Although a man or a woman may keep you last, the King is making your first, if you trust him."
                                    -Inspired by Tina Cooley

"Our faith is greater than our problems."
                                    -Pastor Vincent Ervin

"Look to the Lord and his strength; seek his face always."
-1 Chronicles 16:11

My two cents: It is so easy to get caught up in life living for ourselves and following the crowd. But, when it comes to living our lives for Jesus, it becomes extremely difficult. But, as Les Brown says, "I don't know what the secret to success is, but I know the secret to failure…trying to please everyone."

Notes:
_____
_____
_____

"The most important thing you will ever do in life is to invite Jesus into your heart as your Lord and Savior. The second most important thing is to keep him in that position."
-Inspired by Vivian Johnson

"The man without the spirit does not accept the things that come from the spirit of God for they are foolishness to him and he cannot understand them because they are spiritually discerned. The spiritual man makes judgements about all things but he himself is not subject to any man's judgment."
-1 Corinthians 2:14-15

"Again Jesus spoke to them, saying, "I am the light of the world. Whoever follows me will not walk in darkness, but will have the light of life."
-John 8:12

My two cents: If you were to walk into a room in an unfamiliar house and the entire house was dark, except for one small corner, would you say that you have truly experienced being in that house and know what is has to offer? Yet, if the house was fully illuminated and there was no darkness, would you be able to say that you've experienced what that house had to offer?

Notes:
_____
_____
_____

Acknowledgements:

I would like to thank everyone who helped contribute the many quotes that are included in the book. I am also grateful for my wife, Ashley, for putting up with me while writing this book. It seemed like it was simple, but never-ending. Thank you to all of those individuals that have supported me financially, spiritually, and mentally. Life is tough, especially when you have dreams of making a better life than the one that was provided for you.

For more information about speaking engagements and bookings, or for more products, please feel free to contact us via email at:

Motivatemenow00@yahoo.com

Visit my website for products and services at:
Motivate-me-now.com

Follow me on social media:

Instagram: ReggieDGarland

Twitter: ReggieDGarland

Facebook:
https://www.facebook.com/positivelymotivatingothers/

Citations

[i] *This Made Martin Lawrence A Marked Man By The Illuminati*. By Martin Lawrence. Prod. Arsenio Hall. Perf. Martin Lawrence, Arsenio Hall. YouTube, LLC, 2016. *YouTube*. Web. 19 Dec. 2016.

[ii] Lama, Dalai, XIV. "Dalai Lama XIV Quotes." *Good Reads*. Good Reads, Inc., n.d. Web. 23 Dec. 2016.

[iii] Dr. Seuss. BrainyQuote.com, Xplore Inc, 2017. https://www.brainyquote.com/quotes/quotes/d/drseuss161986.html, accessed April 28, 2017.

[iv] Jim Rohn. BrainyQuote.com, Xplore Inc, 2017. https://www.brainyquote.com/quotes/quotes/j/jimrohn147498.html, accessed March 27, 2017.

[v] Sweetland, Ben. "Quotes about being happy." *Images: happiness*. Google Play, n.d. Web. 14 Jan. 2017.

[vi] Prod. J. Mane. Perf. Leslie C. Brown. YouTube, LLC, 2014. Live Performance. *YouTube.com*. YouTube, LLC, 06 Oct. 2014. Web. 07 Jan. 2017.

[vii] Unknown. "Quotes about being happy." *Dandelionquotes.com*. Google Play, n.d. Web. 16 Jan. 2017.

[viii] Dalai Lama. BrainyQuote.com, Xplore Inc, 2017. https://www.brainyquote.com/quotes/quotes/d/dalailama446740.html, accessed April 30, 2017.

[ix] *What to do when it Stops working, and Life is Changing*. Dir. Bishop T. D. Jakes Sermons. Perf. Bishop T. D. Jakes. *What to do when it Stops working, and Life is Changing*. YouTube, LLC, 30 Oct. 2016. Web. 22 Jan. 2017.

[x] Euripides. BrainyQuote.com, XploreInc, 2017. https://www.brainyquote.com/quotes/quotes/e/euripides149013.html, accessed February 23, 2017.

[xi] Lyndon B. Johnson. BrainyQuote.com, Xplore Inc, 2017. https://www.brainyquote.com/quotes/quotes/l/lyndonbjo103549.html, accessed April 30, 2017.

[xii] Helen Keller. BrainyQuote.com, Xplore Inc, 2017. https://www.brainyquote.com/quotes/quotes/h/helenkelle120988.html, accessed April 30, 2017.

[xiii] Les Brown. AZQotes.com. Wind and Fly LTD, 2017. http://www.azquotes.com/quote/1318274,accessed February 23, 2017.

[xiv] H.Jackson Brown, Jr.. AZQuotes.com. Retrieved March 06, 2017, from AZQuotes.com/quote/566641, accessed March 06, 2017.

[xv] Ausonius. BrainyQuote.com, Xplore Inc, 2017.

https://www.brainyquote.com/quotes/quotes/a/ausonius390441.html, accessed April 30, 2017.

[xvi] John Lennon. AZQuotes.com, Wind and Fly LTD, 2017.
http://www.azquotes.com/quote/41631, accessed April 30, 2017.

[xvii] John F. Kennedy. (n.d.). BrainyQuote.com. Retrieved April 30, 2017, from BrainyQuote.com Web site:
https://www.brainyquote.com/quotes/quotes/j/johnfkenn121068.html.

[xviii] Marie Curie. AZQuotes.com, Wind and Fly LTD, 2017.
http;//www.azquotes.com/quote/517883, accessed March 28, 2017.

[xix] *Prove Them Wrong- Motivational video*. Dir. Be Inspired. *YouTube.com*. YouTube, LLC, 11 Sept. 2015. Web. 11 Jan. 2017.

[xx] Vince Lombardi. (n.d.). AZQuotes.com. Retrieved March 06, 2017, from AZQutoes.com Web site: http://www.azquotes.com/quote/178077.

[xxi] Simmons, Michael. "If You Want To Go Fast, Go Alone. If You Want To Go Far, Go Together." *Entrepreneurs*. Forbes, 22 July 2013. Web. 21 Jan. 2017.

[xxii] *God knows Your Sacrifices and Your Sufferings!!! Take the Cross and Follow HIM*. Dir. Bishop T. D. Jakes. Perf. Bishop T. D. Jakes. *YouTube.com*. YouTube, LLC, 23 Nov. 2016. Web. 14j Jan. 2017.

[xxiii] Frederick Douglass. BrainyQuote.com, XploreInc, 2017.
https://www.brainyquote.com/quotes/quotes/f/frederickd101257.html, accessed February 20, 2017.

[xxiv] Henry Ford. BrainyQuote.com, Xplore Inc, 2017.
https://www.brainyquote.com/quotes/quotes/h/henryford122451.html, accessed March 13, 2017.

[xxv] Dale Carnegie. AZQuotes.com, Wind and Fly LTD, 2017.
http://www.azquotes.com/quote/48670, accessed March 06, 2017.

[xxvi] Milicia, Gina. "A Comfort Zone is a Beautiful Place, But Nothing Ever Grows There." GinaMilicia.com. January 25, 2017. Accessed February 20, 2017. https://ginamilicia.com/2017/01/a-comfort-zone-is-a-beautiful-place-but-nothing-ever-grows-there/.

[xxvii] Milicia, Gina. "A Comfort Zone is a Beautiful Place, But Nothing Ever Grows There." GinaMilicia.com. January 25, 2017. Accessed February 20, 2017. https://ginamilicia.com/2017/01/a-comfort-zone-is-a-beautiful-place-but-nothing-ever-grows-there/.

[xxviii] E. Joseph Cossman. BrainyQuote.com, Xplore Inc, 2017.
https://www.brainyquote.com/quotes/quotes/e/ejosephco120879.html, accessed March 26, 2017.

[xxix] "Perseverance is the hard work you do after you get tired of doing the hard work you already did."

[xxx] https://www.youtube.com/watch?v=8WsVhIN-FSg&t=24s.
[xxxi] Confucius. BrainyQuote.com, Xplore Inc, 2017. https://www.brainyquote.com/quotes/quotes/c/confucius140908.html, accessed March 27, 2017.

[xxxii] Benjamin Disraeli. BrainyQuote.com, Xplore Inc, 2017. https://www.brainyquote.com/quotes/quotes/b/benjamindi154201.html, accessed March 27, 2017

[xxxiii] Avery, Zachary H. "5 Tips to Help Us Get through Anything & 10 Quotes on Perseverance." Elephant Journal: It's about the mindful life. March 24, 2015. Accessed March 28, 2017. https://www.elephantjournal.com/2015/03/5-tips-to-help-us-get-through-anything-10-quotes-on-perseverance/.

[xxxiv] Quotes.net, STANDS4 LLC, 2017. "Hannibal Quotes." Accessed March 27, 2017. http;//www.quotes.net/quote/13956.

[xxxv] George M. Moore, Jr. Braintrainingtools.org, Brainquotes, 2017. http://www.braintrainingtools.org/skills/a-winner-is-just-a-loser-who-tried-one-more-time/, accessed March 27, 2017.

[xxxvi] F. Scott Fitzgerald. BrainyQuote.com, Xplore Inc, 2017. https://www.brainyquote.com/quotes/quotes/f/fscottfit161657.html, accessed March 27, 2017.

[xxxvii] Toren, Matthew. "8 Highly Effective Business Success Tips for Entrepreneurs." *Entrepreneur*, June 4, 2015.

[xxxviii xxxviii] Linkner, Josh. "Want The Thing You've Never Had? Then Do the Thing You've Never Done." Forbes. April 27, 2017. Accessed April 30, 2017. https://forbes.com/sites/chrismyers/2017/04/28/how-to-become-a-more-decisive-leader/#69c78cdd7433.

[xxxix] King, Reverend Dr. Martin Luther, Jr. "Quotes by Martin Luther King." Goodread.com. December 25, 2016. Accessed February 13, 2017. http://www.goodreads.com/quotes/26963-if-you-can-t-fly-then-run-if-you-can-t-run.

[xl] Spencer, Colter, III. "Overcoming-fear-quotes-famous." F5Quotes. February 13, 2017. Accessed February 13, 2017. https://www.f5quotes.com/download/wEuOKKk.

[xli] West, Christina. "...fear quotes and saying to..." F5Quotes. February 13, 2017. Accessed February 13, 2017. https://www.f5quotes.com/download/dmeCH3q.

[xlii] Mandela, Nelson. "Quotes by Nelson Mandela." F5Quotes. February 13, 2017. Accessed February 13, 2017. https://www.f5quotes.com/download/dCNj2fz.

[xliii] Kemmer, Estell. "Fear is one of the biggest..." F5Quotes. February 13, 2017. Accessed February 13, 2017. https://www.f5quotes.com/download/HjGVHZk.

[xliv] Carnegie, Dale . "Dale Carnegie Quotes." ThinkExist.com. February 20, 2017.

Accessed February 20, 2017. http://thinkexist.com/quotation/inaction_breeds_doubt_and_fear-action_breeds/7563.html.

[xlv] Bruce Lee. BrainyQuote.com, XploreInc, 2017. https://www.brainyquote.com/quotes/quotes/b/brucelee383809.html, accessed February 20, 2017.

[xlvi] Bindley, Katherine. "Chesapeake Bay Bridge Drive-Over Company Charges $25 To Anxious Customers." *The Huffington Post*, March 28, 2013. Accessed March 15, 2017. http://www.huffingtonpost.com/2013/05/28/chesapeake-bay-bridge-drive-over_n_3346540.html.

[xlvii] Peter McWilliams. BrainyQuote.com, XploreInc, 2017. https://www.brainyquote.com/quotes/quotes/p/petermcwil125899.html, accessed February 20, 2017.

[xlviii] Dan Millman. BrainyQuote.com, XploreInc, 2017. https://www.brainyquote.com/quotes/quotes/d/danmillman173284.html, accessed February 20, 2017.

[xlix] Martin O'Malley. BrainyQuote.com, XploreInc, 2017. https://www.brainyquote.com/quotes/quotes/m/martinoma701446.html, accessed February 20, 2017.

[l] Alan Watts. AZQuotes.com, Wind and Fly LTD, 2017. http://www.azquotes.com/quote/782753, accessed April 30, 2017.

[li] Plato. BrainyQuote.com, Xplore Inc, 2017. https://www.brainyquote.com/quotes/quotes/p/plato104744.html, accessed March 8, 2017.

[lii] Regina Brett. BrainyQuote.com, Xplore Inc, 2017. https://www.brainyquote.com/quotes/quotes/r/reginabret586778.html, accessed March 8, 2017.

[liii] Wayne Dyer. AZQuote.com, Wind and Fly LTD, 2017. http://www.azquotes.com/quote/499563, accessed March 08, 2017.

[liv] Henry Ford. AZQuotes.com, Wind and Fly LTD, 2017. http://www.azquotes.com/quote/99174, accessed March 19, 2017.

[lv] George Lucas. (n.d.). AZQuotes.com. Retrieved March 28, 2017, from AZQuotes.com Web site: http://www.azquotes.com/quote/408237.

[lvi] Georgette Mosbacher. AZQuotes.com, Wind and Fly LTD, 2017. http://www.azquotes.com/quote/693274, accessed April 04, 2017.

[lvii] Georgette Mosbacher. AZQuotes.com, Wind and Fly LTD, 2017. http://www.azquotes.com/quote/664257. accessed April 04, 2017.

[lviii] Herbert Bayard Swope. AZQuotes.com, Wind and Fly LTD, 2017. http://www.azquotes.com/quote/289027, accessed May 01, 2017.

lix *How To Get What You Want.* Directed by Steinbeck Academy. Performed by Zig Ziglar. YouTube.com. April 09, 2015. Accessed March 27, 2017. https://www.youtube.com/watch?v=rSZZ2m5y4wk&t=2967s.

lx Brown, Carolyn M. "11 Principles to Succeed in Business and Life, from T.D. Jakes." *Black Enterprise- Wealth for Life*, January 12, 2016.

lxi *I Know Who I am*. Directed by T. D. Jakes. Performed by T. D. Jakes. YouTube.com. March 26, 2017. Accessed March 26, 2017. https://www.youtube.com/watch?v=LaxERKoo6kw&t=1885s.

lxii *Dream- Motivational Video*. Directed by Mateusz M. Performed by Les Brown. YouTube.com. June 2, 2013. Accessed March 27, 2017. https://www.youtube.com/watch?v=g-jwWYX7Jlo&t=5s.

lxiii Jim Rohn. AZQuotes.com, Wind and Fly LTD, 2017. http://www.azquotes.com/quote/249607, accessed March 29, 2017.

lxiv Samuel Ullman. AZQuotes.com, Wind and Fly LTD, 2017. http://www.azquotes.com/quote/299794, accessed March 29, 2017.

lxv *Eric Thomas, Motivational Speech, How Bad Do You Want It.* Directed by Nathan Scaglione. Performed by Eric Thomas. YouTube.com. January 22, 2015. Accessed March 29, 2017. https://www.youtube.com/watch?v=6vuetQSwFW8.

lxvi Harriet Tubman. BrainyQuote.com, Xplore Inc, 2017. https://www.brainyquote.com/quotes/quotes/h/harriettub310306.html, accessed March 29, 2017.

lxvii Christopher Reeve. BrainyQuote.com, Xplore Inc, 2017. https://www.brainyquote.com/quotes/quotes/c/christophe141891.html, accessed March 29, 2017.

lxviii Guest, Edgar A. "Don't Quit By Edgar A. Guest." All-creatures.org. January 1, 2017. Accessed March 29, 2017. http://www.all-creatures.org/poetry/dontquit.html.

lxix C. S. Lewis. AZQuotes.com, Wind and Fly LTD, 2017. http://www.azquotes.com/quote/524149, accessed March 30, 2017.

lxx Peter De Vries. AZQuotes.com, Wind and Fly LTD, 2017. http://www.azquotes.com/quote/304052, accessed March 30, 2017.

lxxi Benjamin Franklin. AZQuotes.com, Wind and Fly LTD, 2017. http://ww.azquotes.com/quote/102025, accessed March 30, 2017.

lxxii Shapiro, Fred R. "Who Wrote the Serenity Prayer?" TheChronicle.com. April 28, 2014. Accessed March 30, 2017. http://www.chronicle.com/article/Who-Wrote-the-Serenity-Prayer-/146159.

lxxiii Josh Billings. AZQuotes.com, Wind and Fly LTD, 2017. http://www.azquotes.com/quote/359813, accessed March 29, 2017.

lxxiv Ralph Waldo Emerson. AZQuotes.com, Wind and Fly LTD, 2017.

http://www.azquotes.com/quote/343445, accessed April 05, 2017.
lxxv Washington Irving. AZQuotes.com, Wind and Fly LTD, 2017.
http://www.azquotes.com/quote/141881, accessed April 05, 2017.
lxxvi David Jeremiah. AZQuotes.com, Wind and Fly LTD, 2017.
http://www.azquotes.com/quote/929267, accessed May 01, 2017.
lxxvii *How To Get What You Want*. Directed by Steinbeck Academy. Performed by Zig Ziglar. YouTube.com. April 09, 2015. Accessed March 27, 2017. https://www.youtube.com/watch?v=rSZZ2m5y4wk&t=2967s.
lxxviii Gordon, Jon. *The positive dog: a story about the power of positivity*. Hoboken, NJ: John Wiley, 2012.
lxxix Bob Marley. AZQuotes.com, Wind and Fly LTD, 2017.
http://www.azquotes.com/quote/482335, accessed April 11, 2017.
lxxx Albert Eintein. AZQuotes.com, Wind and Fly LTD, 2017.
http://www.azquoes.com/quote/369328, accessed May 08, 2017.
lxxxi Billy Graham. BrainyQuote.com, Xplore Inc, 2017.
https://www.brainyquote.com/quotes/quotes/b/billygraha150661.html, accessed April 11, 2017.

lxxxii Pablo Neruda. AZQuotes.com, Wind and Fly LTD, 2017.
http;//www.azquotes.com/quote/346023, accessed April 11, 2017.
lxxxiii Max Lucado. AZQuotes.com, Wind and Fly LTD, 2017.
http://azquotes.com/quote347956, accessed April 11, 2017.
lxxxiv Paulo Coelho. AZQuotes.com, Wind and Fly LTD, 2017.
http://azquotes.com/quote/450822, accessed April 11, 2017.
lxxxv Banana Yoshimoto. AZQuotes.com, Wind and Fly LTD, 2017.
http://www.azquotes.com/quote/39400, accessed April 11, 2017.
lxxxvi Laozi. AZQuotes.com, Wind and Fly LTD, 2017.
http://www.azquoes.com/quoe/518236, accessed April 11, 2017.
lxxxvii Nhat Hanh. AZQuotes.com, Wind and Fly LTD, 2017.
http://www.azquotes.com/quote/441275, accessed April 11, 2017.
lxxxviii Sri Chinmoy. AZQuotes.com, Wind and Fly LTD, 2017.
http://ww.azquotes.com/quote/766847, accessed April 19, 2017.
lxxxix Martin Lther King, Jr. AZQuotes.com, Wind and Fly LTD, 2017.
http://www.azquotes.com/quote/158968, accessed April 20, 2017.
xc Desmond Tutu. BrainyQuote.com, Xplore Inc, 2017.
https://www.brainyquote.com/quotes/quotes/d/desmondtut454129.html, accessed April 20, 2017.

xci C. S. Lewis. AZQuotes.com, Wind and Fly LTD, 2017.
http://www.azquoes.com/quote/406131, accessed April 20, 2017.
xcii Anne Roiphe. BrainyQuote.com, Xplore Inc, 2017.
https://www.brainyquote.com/quotes/quotes/a/anneroiphe575179.html, accessed April 21, 2017.

[xciii] Patti Davis. BrainyQuote.com, Xplore Inc, 2017. https://www.brainyquote.com/quotes/quotes/p/pattidavis671740.html, accessed April 21, 2017.

[xciv] Walter Anderson. BrainyQuote.com, Xplore Inc, 2017. https://www.brainyquote.com/quotes/quotes/w/walterande183075.html, accessed April 24, 2017.

[xcv] David A. Bednar. (n.d.). AZQuotes.com. Retrieved April 25, 2017, from AZQuotes.com Web site: http://www.azquotes.com/quote/689155.

[xcvi] Corrie Ten Boom. AZQuotes.com, Windy and Fly LTD, 2017. http://www.azquotes.com/quote/32077, accessed March 05, 2017.

[xcvii] *The Mindset Behind Success*. Directed by Be Inspired. Performed by Connor McGregor, Idris Elba, Denzel Washington, Jon Jones, Jim Carrey, Steve Harvey, Wayne Dyer, Stewart Hughes, T. D. Jakes. YouTube.com. August 1, 16. Accessed March 23, 2017. https://www.youtube.com/watch?v=oG-kWW4um0s.

[xcviii] David Jeremiah. AZQuotes.com, Wind and Fly LTD, 2017. http://www.azquoes.com/quote/908357, access May 02, 2017.

[xcix] Max Lucado. AZQuotes.com. Wind and Fly LTD, 2017. 28 April 2017. http://www.azquotes.com/quote/347662, accessed April 28, 2017.

[c] Gordon, Jon. *The positive dog: a story about the power of positivity*. Hoboken, NJ: John Wiley, 2012.

www.ingramcontent.com/pod-product-compliance
Lightning Source LLC
Chambersburg PA
CBHW042315150426

43201CB00001B/4